WHY DO PUPPIES DO THAT?
REAL THINGS KIDS LOVE TO KNOW

Seymour Simon

PHOTO CREDITS

Permission to use the following photographs is gratefully acknowledged:

Title Page: © Yoshio Tomii / KimballStock; p.3: © Kai Chiang / 123RF; pp. 4, 12, 22 © NaturePL / SuperStock; pp. 6–7, 30 © Ron Kimball / KimballStock; p. 8 © Labat-Rouquette / KimballStock; p. 9 © Ljupco Smokovski / 123RF; p. 11 © Lana Langlois / 123RF; pp. 14, 20, 21, 28–29 © Jane Burton / Photo Researchers, Inc.; p. 16 © Suzi Nelson / Shutterstock; pp. 17, 23 © Blend Images / SuperStock; p. 19 © imagebroker.net / SuperStock; p. 24: © Gary Randall / KimballStock; p. 26 © Brian Kimball / KimballStock; p. 32 © Charles Harbutt.

Why Do Puppies Do That? Real Things Kids Love to Know
Copyright © 2010, 2019 by Seymour Simon. All rights reserved.
Original eBook design by Gordon Whiteside.
Published by Seymour Science LLC

Except in the case of brief quotations embodied in critical reviews and articles, no part of this book may be used or reproduced in any manner whatsoever without written permission from the publisher.
Contact: Great Dog Literary, P.O. Box 456, Craryville, NY 12521

Library of Congress Cataloging-in-Publication Data
Simon, Seymour
Why Do Puppies Do That? Real Things Kids Love to Know / by Seymour Simon
1. Pets — Juvenile literature.
Summary: Fourteen frequently asked questions about puppies. A photo-illustrated introduction to owning and caring for your first pet.
ISBN: 978-0999391297

To Liz
with love and professional admiration

This book is also available as an eBook.
Visit SeymourSimon.com to learn more

Introduction

Getting a puppy is a big decision. Taking care of a puppy takes a lot of time and attention. When puppies grow into adult dogs, they still need love and attention from their owners.

Puppies offer so much in return for your affection. They are great fun to play with and always are ready to be your companion. They can cheer you up when you feel sad or lonely. They have helpful barks that can let you know someone's at the door, or even warn you of danger.

Perhaps best of all, caring for a puppy teaches you the value of loving and being loved.

Why do puppies
bark and yip?

Puppies love to play and be petted. A puppy will try to get your attention when you leave or decide to take a break. That's why she starts to bark, yip, cry, whine, and howl. The puppy is just acting normal. When the barking doesn't work, she may throw a puppy-sized tantrum or even throw up her food.

You should try to ignore a lot of the noise a puppy makes, so she doesn't learn that barking always gets her what she wants. Of course, that's easy to say and harder to do. But ignoring the noise is the best way for you to teach your puppy who's the bark boss in your house!

Why do puppies
wag their tails?

Puppies can't speak in words, but their tails help tell us how they feel. When a puppy wags its tail from side to side, it's a sign that he is happy and friendly. When a puppy is alert and feels threatened, he holds his tail erect and stiff. If the puppy is afraid, his tail goes between his legs. If you watch your puppy, you'll soon learn how a puppy "talks."

If you give your puppy a bowl of food or water, he may wag his tail happily at you. But if the puppy comes to eat or drink at his bowl and no one is around, he won't wag. After all, you don't talk to a dinner plate, so why should your puppy wag his tail at a dinner bowl?

Why do puppies
cry at night?

A new puppy is full of fun when you play with her at home. But then it's late and time for both of you to go to bed. You turn off the lights, and suddenly the fun is over. The puppy begins to cry and whine. All you want to do is sleep, but all your puppy wants to do is cry.

What's different at night? Puppies are lonely for company and attention when no one is around. They often enjoy some soft toys to chew on at sleep time. A loud-ticking clock in a soft sock often comforts a puppy. Once she becomes familiar with her surroundings, a puppy will be able to sleep the whole night.

Why do puppies
tilt their heads?

A puppy will often tilt its head to the side as if he's asking you "What's up?" or "What do you mean?" The puppy looks just like a person who wants to know more (only the puppy is usually more adorable). As soon as a puppy learns words like eat or food, he'll tilt his head without even seeing or smelling the food.

Puppies also tilt their heads to hear sounds. Puppies with big, floppy ears hear better if they tilt their heads so that sounds can pass through their ear flaps more easily.

But sometimes puppies tilt just to get more attention. Those clever little doggies quickly learn that they will get a hug or a treat because they look so cute when they tilt their heads!

Why do puppies **chew on everything?**

Puppies explore the world around them with their mouths, just the way human babies explore things with their mouths. Your puppy may also like to chew on things that have your smell on them because she loves you. Chewing on your shoes is much more fun than chewing on a puppy toy.

Puppies chew the most from about three months to about ten months old, when their permanent teeth start growing. You should teach your puppy to know what she can chew and what she shouldn't. A puppy can be taught by your tone of voice and a reward that chewing on a dog bone is fine, but chewing on the TV remote is a big no-no!

Why do puppies

growl when they play?

Puppies growl when they play, and it's just that —playful growling. It's something like when you were little and pretended to be a superhero. Maybe the puppy is making believe that he is Super Puppy and saving a box of treats from the Dog Biscuit Monster!

While play fighting and growling are perfectly fine for a puppy, it's not acceptable behavior for an adult dog. When a dog growls at someone, it is a threat to the person at whom the dog is growling. He needs to know that he must never growl at you or anyone in your family.

Why do puppies
wet the floor?

Young puppies are bound to make mistakes and wet on the floor when you first bring them home. Puppies are intelligent, but they do not think the way that you do. If you punish a puppy for wetting the floor, she won't understand why you're angry.

Most puppies learn to be paper trained in a few weeks. When you praise a puppy when she wets on the paper, it's like getting a good report card from school. A first-rate puppy also loves to be rewarded with a tasty doggy treat!

Why do puppies bite your fingers?

Puppies normally play fight—bare their teeth and bite their brothers and sisters—and they like to play the same way with you and your family. That's how a puppy develops his physical skills of moving, jumping, and hunting. It's also the way a puppy learns how to act with others in his "pack." Even though your puppy may look fierce, it's just a game for him.

Sometimes puppies bite really hard even when they are playing. They don't know that they can hurt a person when they clamp down on a finger. A smart puppy will quickly learn "Hard biting, no play!"

Why do puppies **play with kittens?**

Puppies and kittens don't always fight "like cats and dogs." Puppies and kittens can become good friends, indifferent neighbors, or constant fighters. It all depends upon the puppy and the kitten and how they are introduced.

If puppies and kittens are raised peacefully together, they will probably get used to each other and even enjoy play fighting together. There are many stories of puppies and kittens that stay friends for life.

Why do puppies
scratch all the time?

Puppies scratch for the same reason that people do—because they itch. A little scratching is normal, especially if the puppy has just had a bath and her skin is dry. A puppy may also scratch more in a heated house or apartment in the winter where the humidity is very low and the air is dry.

More serious scratching problems may be caused by fleas or mites in a puppy's ears or on the skin. Mites or fleas bother a puppy and can cause a lot of itching and scratching. If a puppy scratches herself a lot, it might be time for a trip to the vet.

Why don't puppies sit when they are told?

Puppies don't know how to follow commands just naturally. They have to be taught what to do. The first command a puppy usually learns is "Sit!" But you can't just tell a puppy to sit and expect him to know what you mean. Say "Sit!" in a firm voice and gently push his hindquarters down until he is in the "sit" position. A puppy learns by being praised and rewarded with a doggy treat each time he succeeds.

Sitting is usually an easy command for a puppy to learn. Learning to stay and come is more difficult. Still, the better a puppy is trained, the easier it is to have a dog in the family.

Why do puppies **yawn?**

Puppies yawn for some of the same reasons that you do. They might be tired or bored, or feeling nervous or scared. If a puppy begins to yawn when she's being trained, she probably needs a break.

Yawning is catching. When you're yawning and ready to go to bed, your puppy will yawn right along with you. If your puppy starts to yawn first, you may find yourself suddenly yawning and feeling sleepy!

Why do puppies
whimper while they're sleeping?

Puppies make all kinds of noises when they sleep. They snore, yip, bark, whimper, and growl. Sometimes their legs move just as if they're running.

Your puppy is probably dreaming and responding to something in her dreams, just like you do. This is nothing to worry about, though you may not like the snoring!

Watching a puppy run in her sleep is like watching a video where you can see the hero and not the background. There is no way to know if the puppy is dreaming about fetching a stick or chasing a neighbor's cat.

Why do puppies
lick my face?

30

Dogs and puppies have lived with people for centuries, but many of the things they do, such as licking, are left over from the wild. Puppies lick their mother's mouth so they can feed on partially digested food. You probably won't throw up your food when a puppy licks your face. But it might make you give your puppy a dog biscuit!

Even when your puppy grows up to be an adult, he will lick your face. He thinks you're both in the same pack and licks you to show you respect as the "top dog."

ABOUT THE AUTHOR

Seymour Simon

Seymour Simon, whom the *New York Times* called "the dean of [children's science] writers," is the author of more than 270 highly acclaimed science books, more than 75 of which have been named Outstanding Science Trade Books for Children by the National Science Teachers Association (NSTA). He has also won the *American Association for the Advancement of Science/ Subaru Lifetime Achievement Award* for his lasting contribution to children's science literature, among many other awards.

Seymour Simon's website, SeymourSimon.com, is a unique online destination designed to engage children in reading, writing, and interacting with Seymour and his books, as well as to provide families and educators with a rich array of free, downloadable resources designed to enhance their children's reading experience. The website has been recognized with awards from the Parents Choice® Foundation in 2011 and 2013, was declared an Official Honoree in the Personal Blog/Website category in The *15th Annual Webby Awards*, was named one of twelve "2012 Great Websites for Kids" by the American Library Association, and in 2013 won the QED (Quality-Excellence-Design) Seal of Approval from Digital Book World's *Publishing Innovation Awards*.

Seymour Simon's books encourage children to enjoy the world around them through learning and discovery, and by making science fun. He has introduced tens of millions of children to a staggering array of subjects; one prominent science education specialist described Simon's books as "extraordinary examples of expository prose." Simon taught science and creative writing in elementary and secondary schools and was chair of the science department at a junior high school in the New York City public school system before leaving to become a full-time writer. "I haven't really given up teaching," he says, "and I suppose I never will, not as long as I keep writing and talking to kids around the country and the world."

CPSIA information can be obtained
at www.ICGtesting.com
Printed in the USA
LVHW072203170520
655785LV00008B/391